The Case

for a

Learner's

Charter

for Schools

GUS JOHN

'I have never let my schooling
interfere with my education'
Mark Twain

gus john

with an introduction by

CHRIS SEARLE

First published 2010 by New Beacon Books Ltd.
76 Stroud Green Road, London N4 3EN
for Gus John
www.gusjohn.com

© 2010 Gus John

ISBN 978 1 873201 24 4

Printed by Imprint Digital, Exeter, England

Foreword

Gus John's case for a Learner's Charter for schools is both timely and necessary. He was consulting upon it in the months leading up to the 2010 General Election, a period in which we found each of the major political parties reflecting their intellectual and moral bankruptcy when it comes to developing effective and inclusive state education that enables all our young people to achieve their academic and social potential. Instead they were all introducing variants of increasing marketization, privatization, competition and loss of accountable democratic control. Chris Searle in his introduction develops this analysis and John examines the devastating consequences of this approach over the last 22 years.

International Human Rights Law commits us in the UK to developing effective education for all in inclusive primary and secondary schools. As John points out, a schooling system with 135,000 school age children at any one time out of school, either because they have been excluded or have chosen to stay away, cannot possibly meet this standard and is leading to major social problems in our cities. Further it represents only the tip of the iceberg of failure, with the bottom quartile of the school population falling further behind their hot-housed and over tested peers. The bottom quartile is made up of young people who are white working class, disabled, black Caribbean or from other ethnic minorities. This represents a major social and cultural failure.

The answer is simple, but hard to achieve. It is focused on the involvement of the young people themselves in their education. Not with tokenistic measures such as school councils or Personal, Social and Health Education, but with real involvement based on a meaningful curriculum. This must include an understanding of the struggles to achieve the rights they now have, self knowledge and respect and a curriculum that enables young people to be supported, engaged and encouraged to question and in return grow to take on their social and personal responsibilities.

I first met Gus John on the tenth anniversary of Blair Peach's death in Southall, where he bounded up and told me he had been appointed Director of Education in Hackney and he was looking forward to working with me. I was the NUT General Secretary in the Borough and a teacher at Hackney Downs School. I knew John from the progressive policies he had previously advocated particularly in anti-racist education. However, the pressures from the Council and other officers prevented such a fruitful collaboration and we were often on opposite sides of local disputes, but I believe we both respected each other as educationalists. John certainly valued the book I had recently published with the ILEA *Disability Equality in the Classroom* and gave me a role as advisor on disability equality.

Over the next 20 years, through a variety of roles, I was part of the campaign for an inclusive education system, where all children regardless of their background or impairments could be educated together. We had some success with David Blunkett, as Secretary of State for Education from 1997 to 2001, pushing for a much more inclusive education system. In 2003-2005 I made a five and half hour film, shot in 41 schools, for the Department for Education which showed that children with all types and severity of impairment could be successfully included. This was given the title *Implementing the Disability Discrimination Act in Schools* and sent to all schools. We also found that many of these schools were operating a differentiated behaviour policy which was leading to low or nil exclusions. Teachers often find the most difficult children to include are those with severe behaviour problems because of what has happened to them in their lives. These schools had worked out strategies to become havens for these most at risk young people.

However, the standards agenda which was disconnected from the schools and communities it was supposedly helping, was powered by a much more powerful imperative – the marketization of education. Our primary education has been changed from progressive and child centred, valuing the teacher's professional knowledge to an obsession with SATs, targets and rigid teaching of the 3Rs. Some inspiring and brave teachers have kept a creative curriculum where real learning takes place, but in other schools boys especially have been turned off learning at an early age. Tony Blair was a vocal advocate of General Agreement on Trades and Services [GATS] at the World Trade Organisation, which was intended to open up lucrative public services to private profit. Through a combination of Private Finance Initiative (PFI), Academies, prescriptive literacy and numeracy programmes and league tables, the mantra of choice disguises the money being siphoned off to private profit. Competition has become a by-word for education which instead should be powered by collaboration. There are urgent challenges for us all to live with diversity and in harmony, within the resource limitations of our planet.

At the heart of the Charter, there is a solution for the world to live in peace and within its resources.

In later years, when I was a Governor of Islington Arts and Media School (IAMS), I was on a platform with John for the Anti Academies Alliance. At IAMS we had turned round a so called 'failing school' without gimmicks, by trusting and supporting our pupils, parents, teachers and mentors, appointing a dynamic head who believed in comprehensive education and protecting our school community from the Government, local council and OFSTED.

In the present period, John's Charter is a breath of fresh air and an exciting initiative. It provides a means for all those who believe in and wish to fight for a properly funded, locally accountable and inclusive education system to come together. Through involving the most important elements in education – the school students and their parents, together with teachers and governors, trade unions and the local community, we can form an alliance to put the Charter into practice and campaign to put in place the political changes needed to ensure a positive future for all our young people. More importantly, we can also empower and include our alienated and excluded young people regardless of race, gender, social class, ethnic background or religion, sexual orientation, impairment or ability, to halt the violence and wastage of life of gang culture in the 'road' and begin to create the sort of society in which we are happy to bring up our children.

I am privileged to have met Gus John again and feel enthused by his educational and human vision. I commend this Charter to all who care about education and equality.

Richard Rieser
Inclusive education consultant and director of World of Inclusion
Member of the NUT

Preface

The idea of a Learner's Charter arose primarily from a series of discussions with school students and their parents as part of my work with the Communities Empowerment Network (CEN). The idea was reinforced as a result of work with learning mentors and teaching assistants in primary and secondary schools in London and elsewhere. Those staff are invariably the ones with whom children share their experience of classroom culture, of the learning environment generally, of the behaviour of their peers and of the way teachers operate. They experience children as being candid about their difficulties in managing themselves in school and about the way their own conduct helps to create those difficulties. But they also see numerous examples of the unfairness and lack of respect with which children and their parents are treated by schools.

For their part, some of those students are high performers and are highly regarded by their peers and by the school community generally. Some are confident learners who nevertheless struggle with the regime of schooling, with the way they are treated by some of their teachers, and with the low expectations many of their peers have of themselves. They worry that some of their peers perform below their ability level out of choice, because it is not seen as 'cool' to be bright and a high achiever. Their experience of secondary schooling in particular leads them to believe that schools have low expectations of black students generally, and of black boys in particular. The black students shared anecdotes about the number of times they handed in brilliant pieces of work of which they were very proud, only to have that work thrown back at them with the accusation that they did not do the work themselves.

Some of those students admit to being poor at managing their own behaviour and dealing with the disruptive tendencies of others; they therefore find themselves at risk of exclusion, or are labelled by their peers and their teachers alike as people from whom aggravation rather than focused learning could be expected. All have had cause to complain about the lack of fairness with which schools deal with students, whether in relation to punishing students from a particular ethnic group more harshly than others, dealing in stereotypes and shaping their expectations on the basis of those stereotypes, or making decisions about setting and streaming.

All bemoan the fact that there are hardly any opportunities created for them to discuss these issues amongst themselves as a learning community, let alone with teachers and school managers.

They are bewildered by the number of initiatives the government introduces under the banner of raising achievement and improving school effectiveness. They worry about the increased pressure those initiatives put upon them and upon their teachers. Above all, they are frustrated that nobody ever consults them and that they have no say in how politicians choose to organize schools and make demands on teachers, students and parents.

They view the flurry of new education legislation and new types and governance of schools with growing cynicism. In one discussion session, a fourteen year old student said: 'I went straight to a new academy in Year 7 and it's the nicest building I have ever been in. It is very strict and there's no messing about. But, more children get excluded from this school than from the one it replaced and when parents support their children, they are treated worse than the students themselves by the headteacher and staff'. An undergraduate student training to be a teacher noted that at a national conference on school exclusions five years earlier, the group he was in had shared similar views, i.e., 'that despite all that new legislation, schooling outcomes and the experience of schooling for the same groups of students, black, mixed race and white working class, were little changed. The same groups of children and young people are favoured by the system and the same groups, visible by class and colour, are soon identified and labelled as the present and future failures'.

If I were to sum up in one sentence the views and the feelings of the students, parents and learning mentors involved in those discussions, it would be this: *It is time for school students to organize themselves and with the support of their parents and teachers reclaim education and rescue schooling.*

The Case for a Learner's Charter is meant to encourage a debate about what schooling is for and how schooling provision should be made, and schools organized and funded, to ensure that **every child does matter** and that schooling contributes to the rounded development of children with confidence, self worth, values and skills that make them fit for living in civil society and contributing to the social and economic life of the community.

For too many children, schooling is a massive irrelevance and both the regime of schooling and the curriculum fail to engage with the matters that preoccupy them in their living outside school.

The challenge, then, is how to make schooling relevant, how to address in schools the burning issues that young people take into schools from their homes, their peer groups and their communities and make sure that teachers have both the competence and the time and resources to deal with them.

That is why a Learner's Charter is so important. That is why the charter I propose is not just framed within the context of the rights of the child, but articulates the entitlements as well as the responsibilities of students themselves, of their families/carers and of schools and teachers.

There is no doubt that the greatest single determinant of a person's experience of schooling is the quality of their learning at the interface between them and their teachers, and the quality of the sharing and learning that define their interactions with their fellow students. Throughout the history of schooling in all societies, caring, capable and committed teachers have transformed the lives and enhanced the life chances of many a student who might otherwise have drifted into hopelessness and been rendered redundant in society. Schools cannot solve all of society's ills, nor should they be expected to. But when all else and everyone else have failed young people, it is the teacher who refuses to write them off and who continues to believe in them and their potential and to invest them with self worth that is often their life line. In every generation and in every society there are many who in adult life bear testimony to that.

Let us all, therefore, use the Learner's Charter to fight for the space, the time and the class size that would make it possible for teachers and schools to perform that key function with and for all children, and especially for those from historically disadvantaged groups, and break this seemingly endless cycle of educational betrayal and a journey into hopelessness.

Here, I make the case for a Learner's Charter and on the basis of exchanges with school students, parents and teachers, I provide suggestions as to what the charter might contain. This is therefore very much a work in progress.

I invite you to use this document to inform a debate about schooling and to send your comments and your suggestions so that the charter could be constructed on the basis of contributions from as large a body of school students, families and teachers as possible.

Gus John
15 February 2010

Introduction

Yesterday morning, as I travelled to work on the Transpennine Express between Sheffield and Manchester, many of the commuters' faces were sunk into the front page headline of their free Metro. 'Teachers face violence daily!' it exclaimed, with a leader of the Association of Teachers and Lecturers raging about 'violence and intimidation from pupils as young as five because of a collapse in classroom behaviour', with teachers 'worrying about having their teeth knocked out and even suffering sexual assault in their classrooms'. Parents of such children should have 'their child benefits payment cut,' she declared, 'and made to attend child parenting classes if their children keep misbehaving at school'.

This is England in 2010 and it is an accurate expression of how low and desperate the educational discourse across the nation has become. It is also a clear signal to school students of all ages, their teachers and parents about the urgent need for debate and action around education that the Learner's Charter advocates. For on the eve of a General Election all three 'mainstream' political parties are commending policies which will only radically worsen the situation in schools, with 'solutions' of increased authoritarianism, arbitrariness and student exclusion, and a faster and faster discarding and dissolution of the public sphere in state education. While New Labour stands for more 'academies' and 'trust schools' to replace comprehensive schools – particularly in the inner cities, with governance increasingly removed from public accountability with school control under the power of unelected and quasi-religious diktat, the Conservative response is the creation of more state-financed 'independent' schools run by self-selected bodies and headteachers with much greater powers to exclude, with the shadow schools minister Michael Gove, speaking of a 'rocket booster' to speed up the existing 'academies' programme. As for the Liberal Democrats, they continue to show their priorities by closing invaluable community-driven schools in cities like Sheffield, where they control council budgets and resources. And all this in the nation where competitive testing and a system of continuous examinations is the most intense in Europe, blighting the objectives of schools of giving to our children an understanding of a humane, cooperative and sharing society and a true preparation for life as it needs to be lived for the betterment and very survival of our world.

The Learner's Charter offers students, parents and teachers a rich opportunity to discuss and analyse education in British schools, focusing upon the issues most pertinent to us all. As a genuine provocation to debate, there is nothing fixed or indelible about its formulations; everything is there to be considered, dissected, reviewed, amended or reconceptualized around its founding principles of inclusion, social justice and equality of provision, and its stimulus to create schools which will enable all the young people of our country 'to take control of their own lives and, as active citizens, have regard for their duties and responsibilities, as well as their rights'.

Yet the Charter is published at a crucial time, where after more than a century of most schools being under, at least theoretically, the accountable control of Local Education Authorities, they are being systematically privatized by a New Labour government. For how do you transform a struggling inner city school into a vibrant and successful learning institution – a question that challenges us all? The New Labour answer is to stop calling it a school and rename it an academy, take it away from any public accountability and give anti-democratic control of it to a group of privateers – business, or Christian evangelistic and other religious sponsors – thus removing its secular status in the process. The ruling sponsors are then allowed to construct their own admissions, disciplinary and curriculum rules and procedures and rob the state economy, with public money paying for the 'academy's' upkeep after the state has received but a measly percentage of its initial capital cost from the sponsors, who retain complete control, waiving teachers' hard-earned rights and treating them as nothing but a new breed of pedagogic servants, completely at their beck and call. 'If academies are to succeed', declared John Burn, ex-academy principal and now 'academic adviser' to the Emmanuel Schools Foundation owned by car salesman Peter Vardy, which currently controls 'academies' in Gateshead, Middlesbrough and Doncaster, 'they need to be led and staffed by people who are obedient to God's truth as revealed in the scriptures'.

It is within these same inner cities that, despite the accumulated brainpower and cosmopolitan genius of their children and the committed work of thousands of teachers, the remnants of backward genetic determinism still remain, stoked by the false sciences of psychometrics and eugenics. High profile pseudo-scientists like Hans Eysenck, Arthur Jensen and their contemporary adherent, James Watson, have identified lower 'inborn' intelligence with black and working class children. This is a tendency continued by New Labour educationalists in their emphasis upon, and championing of, a selected elite of 'gifted' children, complete with 'centres of excellence' and the 'National Academy for Gifted and Talented Youth', to the exclusion of the unselected and ungifted majority.

It needs to be said that educational ideas in Britain are at a profoundly low ebb, with most so-called new insights or educational initiatives being but reversals or re-introductions of failed historical precedents. Despite the enormous efforts of many teachers, the curriculum still remains largely exclusive and unrepresentative of Britain's fast-growing, ultra-diverse and hybrid schools population, particularly in the urban areas where it is most strongly rooted. The sense of alienation, cognitive distrust and irrelevance which thousands of young people feel within their schools is frequently a reflection of curriculum aversion. Who would want to put their heart and brain into studying a continuous body of knowledge which speaks nothing of your people's lives, their achievements, cultures and histories, which still tells outright lies about their very reality? 'My normally sealed educational prison', is how one teenage boy described his school and its curriculum. Yet such is the daily dose of knowledge of our young urban people. Little wonder the underlying anger, resentment and hostility stoked in their minds when they consider the absence of living connection with a curriculum which excludes them and says so little that is real or positive about their lives.

There are, of course, many different models of schooling which tell alternative narratives about daily education. 'Education Studies' would be an engrossing subject for secondary schools, classes which tell of the ideas, practices and realities of schools across the world. It might also prove to be a subject brimming with critical thought. For if young people themselves were to read and share the experiences of others in schools elsewhere that are radically different from the British state model – which is still largely a mass-based emulation of the nineteenth-century British public school with its hierarchies, authoritarianism, curriculum exclusion and Britishness which was also exported unchanged across the British Empire – it might give them the basis of an apprenticeship in criticism and self-criticism which is at the centre of a truly humane and civilizing education. Think of the schools they could study: from the non-conformist models in Britain from Summerhill, Risinghill and the Burston Strike School; to the essential texts about schools in changing times from Makarenko's 'The Road to Life'; to the experiences of the School of Barbiana in Tuscany; from accounts of the transformations in Cuban schools as set down in Karen Wild's 'Children of Che' or Jonathan Kozol's 'Children of the Revolution'. Such invaluable school perspectives would spark many an original and practical insight amongst those who discussed them.

It was a remarkable teacher of Brazil, Paulo Freire, who wrote: 'To the extent that individual freedom is exaggerated, we fall into anarchy. To the extent that externally imposed discipline is exaggerated, we fall into authoritarianism. The answer lies in the equation of freedom and discipline.' Wise words which could trigger many a further discussion about school life. For certainly one of the founding qualities of the Learner's Charter is the precedence that it gives to the voices and ideas of school students, who have been all but excluded from the last fifty years of debate about their schooling, with the exception of the blaze of activity in the early 1970s by the Schools Action Union and the National Association of School Students. In 2006 the school students of Chile organized their own national school students' strike, securing important changes in the life of their schools which still reflected the values and habits of three decades of Pinochet's fascist government. Their national struggle secured them meetings with their President and top government officials and signalled progressive changes in school organization, curriculum and ethos. These were brave actions which called to mind the British schoolchildren's strike of 1911, the protest actions by the children of Soweto against South African apartheid in 1976 and the daily resistance of Palestinian youth against the Israeli occupying army across their land and cities, including the closure of their schools.

The focus upon the human rights of those at school is essential to the Learner's Charter's content, and its reflection of the unequal and dangerous lives lived by millions of English children, among them the 135,000 who are compulsorily excluded or have chosen to exclude themselves by persistent truancy from school life. What future for them, subject to the criminal pressures of street, gang or drug culture? And what present, living without the protection and stimulus for an understanding of life that school should offer? As the ex-headteacher of an inner city comprehensive school which developed the first non-permanent exclusion policy in England, I learned fast how difficult it is to sustain such a policy when a significant sector of the teaching staff were reluctant to implement it, despite the high degree of support it received from school governors and community. For in every major British city there are significant numbers of excluded students whose only school is the street or the shopping mall, removed from their right to state education and protection, with blatantly disproportionate numbers of black and Asian young people among them, their ages becoming younger and younger year by year.

And their cities are becoming more and more dangerous, with the threat of serious harm and death closer to them. Last year I compiled a book of poems by Manchester secondary school students about their city, as a tribute anthology to the ideas and activism of Nelson Mandela on his ninetieth birthday. I was astonished by the poems that emerged from the poetry workshops I taught, with large numbers of the poets expressing their fear of violent street crime and death. One poet, Francis, wrote about his city:

I am the corner which cuts through your flesh
I am the mourner that's put through the test
I am the killer that hides the knife
I am the reaper that thinks death is rife
But most of all, I am the city, the dangerous place
In which you are judged by religion and race.

An anonymous poet put it this way:

Knives are supposed to be for cutting vegetables
not for ruining families

and Tasmiah has waking dreams of a sleep without worry:

How can I sleep at night
Knowing there's gun crime?
How can I sleep at night

Knowing violence is taking over the world?
How can I sleep at night
Knowing people are full of sorrow?
How can I sleep at night
Knowing racism is there?
One day, soon, I know
I will get a good night/s sleep.

All their worries must be openly expressed, discussed and allayed.
School is for that too.

My hope is that this Learner's Charter will become a tool for the discussion of everything pertaining to the lives of children, and used directly within schools, community venues, universities and everywhere where people meet. It is a document of signal relevance, continuing the nineteenth century tradition of the Charter as a prime expression of popular opinion, will and dedication to justice that can become a harbinger of mass activism and campaigning.

But a word about its author, a significant Chartist of our times. When I think of Gus John, born in Grenada in the Caribbean in 1945, I think of the revolutionary tradition of that comparatively small island of slightly over 100,000 people which has produced outstanding figures such as Julien Fedon who led an island-wide revolt against British colonialism in 1795; Tubal Uriah 'Buzz' Butler, organizer of the Trinidadian oilworkers strike in 1936; and John's contemporary and school mate Maurice Bishop, leader of the Grenada Revolution from 1979–1983. Yet I also remember the black British Chartist militant and tailor, William Cuffay, the son of slaves in St Kitt's, born in Chatham, Kent in 1788, 'a scion of Africa's oppressed race' whose defiant years of campaigning for the Charter resulted in his conviction and eventual transportation for life in 1849. He died in a workhouse in Tasmania in 1870, aged 82, a real British hero. Gus John continues that tradition with his Learner's Charter of 2010, carrying the same optimism and democratic longing of Cuffay, of whom a contemporary wrote that his boundless energy would in time overturn 'the darkness of the present time and render more intense the glowing light of the future'.

Chris Searle
Director of the Ahmed Iqbal Ullah Centre, University of Manchester

THE CASE FOR A LEARNER'S CHARTER FOR SCHOOLS

London May 2009

1.0   Why we need a Learner's Charter

1.1   Context

A.

- The School effectiveness and raising attainment agenda
- The Government's commitment to give young people more say in the processes and decisions that affect them
- Learners' educational entitlement
- Personalized learning
- Distributed leadership
- Curriculum relevance and ownership
- The Academies programme
- Government proposals to empower parents to establish schools

B.

i)   International Human Rights Standards

- The best interests of the child must be paramount (Article 3)
- Children have a right to be heard (A.12)
- Children have a right not to be discriminated against on the basis of, for example, class, race, ethnicity, religion/faith or gender (A.2)
  (OR because of the failings of either parent)
- Children have the right to be protected from all forms of violence. They must be kept safe from harm. They must be given proper care by those looking after them. (A.19)

ii)   The canon of equality legislation

iii) The 'Community Cohesion' agenda

iv) The consultation on giving children and young people a right to appeal decisions regarding exclusions, SEN statements and assessments, and to make disability discrimination claims in England

C.

Twelve basic propositions:

i) The primary and ultimate purpose, the Alpha & Omega, of schooling and education is to humanize society.

ii) Schools are being overloaded with initiatives which are incoherent add-ons and which do not add up to a societal consensus on what we want schooling and education to be about.

iii) The education of children is too important for it to become a ready-made canvas on which government applies whatever fancy ideas it might have, while requiring teachers to bend their professionalism and square it with those ideas and the ideology that gives rise to them.

iv) Schooling is still characterized by the structured omission of issues to do with ideology, exploitation, power, discrimination, inequality and social injustice.

v) Whether we teach Religious Studies or Quantum Physics, we do not occupy neutral, non-ideological space, nor are we simply engaging in neutral 'knowledge transfer' activity.

vi) It is the duty of schools to ensure that irrespective of the disposition or beliefs of parents, children and young people are provided with the knowledge, understanding and skills to be at ease with and respect themselves so that they can respect others, especially people who are different from themselves.

vii) The context of schooling in today's Britain is:

a. a multiethnic, multifaith and multiclass society in which *inequality* is as much part of the diversity of the society as is 'race', disability, gender, age, etc.

b. a society impacted by globalization and the many challenges it poses, not least for countries and regions that have a poor record of international activity, multilingualism and intercultural education. In such contexts, globalization is seen as a challenge to social cohesion and regional if not national identity and causes moral panic about the very concept of multiculturalism.

viii) Schooling is increasingly hitched to a neo-liberal agenda that defines its purpose mainly in relation to labour market needs and the nation's economic competitiveness in a global, free-market economy; an ideology that:

- provides the justification for government's obsession with league tables and for school admissions procedures and practices that are potentially discriminatory
- promotes the cult of the individual, selfishness, greed and the 'survival of the fittest', while at the same time espousing 'commonly shared values', as if such values are a given and we could make the assumption that everyone would subscribe to them
- encourages families to buy quality education in the marketplace, rather than acting collectively to ensure that there is 'a good school for every child in every community'
- encourages a situation where seeking private – and privatized – solutions to public ills becomes its own justification

ix) Children need a charter for schooling that will enshrine their entitlements and their responsibilities as learners and provide a framework for those who facilitate their learning and self development.

x) Such a charter would mirror the purpose and intent of the Equity and Diversity agenda and make combating discrimination and social exclusion, promoting equity, diversity and community cohesion organic to what schools do, rather than as yet another set of challenges overburdened teachers are expected to meet.

xi) The charter will be a holistic package and implementation tool for placing the Equality Duty and the Community Cohesion requirements at the very core of what schools do and how children and families relate to the globalized world about them.

xii) The charter places schooling in the driving seat of education for democratic citizenship and enshrines the principle that empowering the individual to develop his/her capacity to act in a self-directing way and to take collective action with others in pursuit of change is at the very heart of the process of managing and expanding a democratic culture.

1.2   Which learner?
       This charter applies to all children, students and families, any
       and everywhere in the country, irrespective of ethnicity, social
       background, impairment, or ability level

1.3   What is its purpose?
   - It aims to focus school students on their identity and purpose as
     learners and as people developing emotionally, spiritually,
     morally, socially, academically and culturally
   - It is meant to assist the learner in developing self confidence,
     insight and emotional literacy and situating him/herself in the
     learning community and in society as an active citizen
   - It is meant to assist learners in understanding, sharing and
     living the values that bind the learning community and the
     wider community together
   - It is meant to guide teachers and families/carers in engaging
     with young people's personal, social and emotional develop-
     ment as well as assisting them in developing political literacy.

1.4   How will it be used?
   - By individual learners as an individual learning and personal
     development 'manifesto' to form the basis of their contract with
     the school and with themselves as learners through their
     individualized learning and personal development plan
   - By teachers and families/carers to support learners in
     constructing and following their plan and in planning their own
     contribution to the learner's personal and academic development
   - By early years practitioners and teachers in curriculum
     planning and delivery such that the objectives of activities and
     lessons reflect learning outcomes consistent with the various
     elements of the charter
   - By taking advantage of the flexibility the National Curriculum
     now gives teachers to go ahead and devise learning packages in
     collaboration with learners and in relation to the many currently
     neglected aspects of their development
   - By learners, teachers and families/carers in monitoring
     learners' progress in meeting the objectives and targets set out
     in the learner's development plan.

2.0   Promoting children-centred schooling and education

2.1   It is time for school students to organize themselves and with the support of their parents and teachers reclaim education and rescue schooling.

2.2   On 31 October 2007, Gordon Brown made a speech at the University of Greenwich in which he shared his intention to create a 'world-class' education system in Britain, settling no more for 'second best':

> *Our ambition must be nothing less than to be world class in education and to move to the top of the global education league, and it is time to say not just that we will aim high but that we can no longer tolerate failure, that it will no longer be acceptable for any child to fall behind,*
>
> *...no longer acceptable for any school to fail its pupils, no longer acceptable for young people to drop out of education without good qualifications without us acting...So no more toleration of second best in Britain, no more toleration of second best for Britain.*
> <http://webarchive.nationalarchives.gov.uk/+/http://www.number10.gov.uk/Page13675>

2.3   Mr Brown's speech was full of catchy sound bites, full of statements that sounded entirely reasonable if not radical. He talked about social justice for all, delivering services that are personal to each but shaped by people themselves, merit of each in the service of all, a decent school and a decent education as an entitlement, education as the key to social progress, the need to raise boys' aspirations, personalized learning and testing and the Government's intention to establish 400 new academies, 150 of them by 2010. He shared parents' concerns about 'discipline, about bullying, about schools where children's lessons are disrupted, and where there is not enough of a school ethos for learning to flourish and all children to succeed', arguing that:

> *If we ask parents to get more involved in the education of their children, in the lives of their schools, we have to respond to these concerns, just as parents for their part need to reinforce the*

> *expectations for good discipline and the boundaries of acceptable behaviour set by head teachers for their schools. So, let us do more now to involve and engage parents at every stage of the journey of their children's education.*

2.4 What is significant about that speech is that despite Brown's claim that children have an 'entitlement' to a decent school and a decent education, he made no reference whatsoever to involving them in any form of consultation on his proposals or to engaging with them in devising strategies to bring about that 'world class' education.

2.5 There have been numerous government initiatives aimed at reforming and restructuring schooling in England and Wales in the last two decades, beginning with the Education Reform Act 1988. Those have ushered in, among other things, local management of schools, academies, non-denominational foundation schools and a range of school improvement programmes including: raising achievement, aiming higher, gifted and talented and much more besides. In addition, schools are mandated to deliver the citizenship curriculum and to engage with the community cohesion agenda.

2.6 The principal focus of these initiatives has been upon:
- extending parental power
- curtailing the power of local authorities to intervene in the management of schools and in schools' admission arrangements, thus displacing the crucial role of elected government in guaranteeing the defence of the individual learner against invidious forces that do not necessarily respect the rights and entitlements of those who cannot fend for themselves, or who constitute the excluded in society
- giving schools wider powers to exclude students, and
- testing, examinations and 'naming and shaming' schools for poor test and examination results, a process that has untold impact upon and induces hopelessness in the children who had no choice but to attend those schools, as well as those teachers – to be found in every such school – who worked hard to overcome the in-built barriers to quality teaching and learning

2.7 Significantly, however, the process of schooling reform both before and since 1988 has largely ignored the one group of people who are meant to be the beneficiaries of those reforms, namely learners themselves. They remain the passive subjects, or victims, of one education lobby after another, one new initiative after another, one change in practice after another, one pedagogical shift after another even when the overt intention may be otherwise. Yet, they are systematically excluded from the debate about school improvement, school governance, the quality of schooling outcomes and what to do about education provision for the 135,000 children of compulsory school age (the equivalent of the roll of 132 large secondary schools) who are out of school, typically because they have been excluded or have voted with their feet and for whom learning provision otherwise than at school needs to be made.

2.8   Mr Brown's agenda for schooling and education is silent on the vexing issues of admissions, school exclusions, legal compliance in relation to the rights of students with SEN and the canon of equality and human rights legislation. It ignores what the national picture is telling us about the operation of the above rights:

- 9,000 permanent exclusions per year in English schools
- 350,000+ fixed term exclusions averaging 3.5 days each
- 14 million days lost through truancy
- Staff sickness absence averaging 5 days per year or 7 times the rate of pupil absence through truancy
- Stress remains a major factor in staff sickness rates

2.9   Where does all of this feature on the agenda of the 'flagship' academies that receive, on average, £1,600 more per pupil from the DCSF than neighbouring comprehensives? Why are the 135,000 school age children who are the focus of the government's 'Back on Track' programme not considered to be similarly worth £1,600 more per pupil?

2.10 Teaching and non-teaching staff in schools are typically organized in trade unions, professional associations and various networks. There are parent teacher associations, parent lobbies, organized parents groups and voluntary education projects. But apart from students councils in schools, which are not independently organized student forums, there are no independent student organizations acting to promote students' education entitlements and safeguard their interests, save for the National Association of School Students which is still in its infancy and has yet to see the development of a significant number of local associations of school students, especially in urban education.

2.11 The schooling debate tends to be about improvement or otherwise in school examination results on the one hand, and disruptive, undisciplined and underperforming students on the other. It is a debate that often fails to compare like with like, dismisses considerations of class, culture, geographical environment and parents' ability to exercise, if not buy, choice of school. The preoccupation with disruptive, undisciplined and underperforming students is part of a wider construction of 'youth' in society , with a focus on anti-social behaviour and ASBOs, under age drinking, teenage pregnancies, youth crime, street violence, inadequate parenting and inadequate parents, and government and schooling interventions that are principally about league tables and about exclusion and punishment.

2.12 This charter is also based upon the premise that while no child has the right to obstruct the learning of others or of teachers' attempts to facilitate that learning, children do not forfeit their educational entitlement on account of their poor self management and discipline. Moreover, it is as much the purpose of schooling to support them in unlearning inappropriate behaviours and acquiring the values, insight and social skills that make them fit for living in civil society and enable them to act as socially adjusted members of the learning community, as it is to help them gain 5 + A*-C grades at GCSE.

2.13 Initiatives such as 'Sure Start', parenting education classes, extended schools and mentoring for young people are all meant to impact upon the way children are guided and supported in their personal and academic development. Such initiatives and those who evaluate them, however, have a tendency to problematize families in certain communities as having an inadequate 'home learning environment' and poor parenting skills. Moreover, they fail to take account of the fact that parents from higher socio-economic groups pay hundreds of pounds per week for early years provision, employ nannies to look after children and pay £50 to £65 per hour for private tuition for primary and secondary age children.

2.14 Michael Gove, then shadow Education Secretary, promised to expand the 'extended schools' programme in order to help children from disadvantaged homes if the Conservatives win the general election. He told the Association of Teachers and Lecturers (ATL) annual conference in Manchester at Easter in 2010 that the Conservatives will introduce Saturday morning classes for such children. 'Children who come from homes where parents don't have the resources to provide additional stretch and cultural experiences could benefit from being in school for longer', he said. 'I believe there is a case for school on Saturday morning to help stretch children ... My hunch is that families would prefer there to be longer hours. Parents would love to have schools starting earlier and certainly love school to be going on later to fit in with their working lives.'

2.15 Gove is right to acknowledge the part played by 'additional stretch' in determining schooling outcomes. Such additional inputs have become the norm for an ever expanding section of the schooling population, with some parents paying up to £60 per hour for after school and weekend tuition for their children. However, he fails to acknowledge that the African heritage community built a national Saturday/Supplementary School movement since the 1960s. Concerned about the miseducation of their children, African-Caribbean parents and community groups established Saturday schools and ran Easter and Summer schools with two principal objectives: one, to provide children with knowledge and guidance about themselves and their background to help build positive identity and counteract the negative attitudes the society displayed towards them and encouraged them to have towards themselves and people who looked like them, and two, to remedy the poor teaching and low expectations that were leading to educational failure for far too many of them year on year.

2.16 A variation of this community based provision, in the form of mother tongue classes or/and instruction about the tenets and tradition of belief systems such as Judaism, Hinduism and

Islam, was to be found among other ethnic groups and faith communities across Britain.

2.17   Why is it that this history of self organization by black and global majority people on the question of schooling and tackling underachievement does not even get a mention from Gove, despite the tens of thousands of school students whose life chances have been preserved and extended by committed teachers in the Saturday/Supplementary School movement? Maybe it is because our contribution to shaping schooling and education in the last fifty years has largely been written out of the social history of Britain to the extent that governments during that period, no less than schools themselves, have acted as if they have or had nothing to learn from what our experience was saying about the British schooling system. One of the many messages we have been at pains to convey to the education establishment is that getting good exam grades is not the sole purpose of schooling and education. As Mark Twain famously said: 'I have never let my schooling interfere with my education'. Another is that decades of antiracist teacher education appear to have done little to eliminate the discrimination suffered by black and white working class students as a result of teachers' low expectations based on race and class. A third is the correlation between teachers' low expectations, the low expectations too many students have of themselves, and poor student behaviour; a mix that accounts in part for the large number of exclusions among African Caribbean boys.

2.18   Before becoming director of education in Hackney in 1989, I was head of community education in the Inner London Education Authority (ILEA) and in charge of the playcentre and youth services. I made it my mission to ensure that those were not childminding services that simply provided social care for children until their parents finished work. The ILEA had a structured system of playcentres and community education classes operating end-on to the school day. School students not only learnt through organized play. They learnt the skills of cooperation, team working, negotiation, problem solving and constructive criticism of self and others. Above all, they learnt the values that informed those processes and how to give those values expression in all aspects of their daily living. Their learning and social education was facilitated by playcentre workers, youth workers, artists, dramatists and parents from a wide variety of backgrounds and occupations. All of those opportunities for non-formal social education and cultural, moral and academic development were debunked once Margaret Thatcher abolished the ILEA. As more and more government funding for education was given directly to schools and colleges, such extended provision for primary age children and youth service/community education provision for secondary was also phased out by many local authorities outside London.

2.19 The contribution such provision makes in helping children to become more confident learners and to develop social skills, insight and emotional literacy is increasingly undervalued. Rather, extended schools both as a Labour government initiative and as proposed by Michael Gove for the Conservatives are seen very much as complementary, if not remedial, to the same fare that children get in the course of the regular school day and are geared primarily to enabling children to achieve better test and examination results.

2.20 Gove is promising a form of social engineering that focuses on enhancing individual achievement and closing the gap between the extra investment in their children's academic success that 'the better off' make and the absence of such investment by parents of 'poorer pupils'. The 'better off' widen the gap even though they make sure their children attend the best schools available, often by finding all sorts of creative ways of securing accommodation within the catchment of those schools. Gove's recipe of 'extended stretch', primarily in preparation for tests and examinations, will do little to tackle the gross inequalities in the provision of schooling, even assuming that a Conservative Government would be able to fund, let alone persuade teachers to take on, those extra evening and weekend duties. The Labour Government's model that involves providing one-to-one tuition for the pupils the Conservatives have in their sights belongs to the same bag.

2.21 'Every Child Matters' and the 2004 Children Act will continue to mean nothing if government (of whichever political colour) does not commit to tackling the structural inequality in schooling by ensuring that there is a good school for every child in every community as a fundamental right. 'Every Child Matters' must surely mean that children are allowed to be children and to explore and derive learning from activities and social interactions that are not focused on passing exams. Children should therefore expect not to have to use their evenings and weekends as an extension of the school timetable.

2.22 Despite the plethora of policies, reforms and initiatives since 1988 that have been geared towards school effectiveness and raising attainment, the last decade has seen the unprecedented rise in the number of young people being murdered by other young people, the number of young people in young offender institutions and in the care of the Youth Offending Service and the number of school age children who are out of school.

2.23 The Department for Children, Schools and Families is rolling out its 'Back on Track' programme with the aim of 'modernizing alternative provision' for the 135,000 young people of compulsory school age in alternative provision, including pupil referral units, in England. The central plank of this programme is the commissioning of such provision from private and voluntary sector organizations and the vetting, registration and accreditation of such providers.

2.24 This is happening at the same time as the government is spending billions on an unprecedented and long overdue 'Building Schools for the Future' programme. Government is therefore institutionalizing a twin track schooling system, with expensive and well appointed schooling facilities for some and considerably less resource intensive provision for the 135,000 young people whom schools have rejected or who have turned their backs on mainstream schooling. All of this is taking place five years after the government replaced the 1989 Children Act with the 2004 Children Act and 'Every Child Matters – Change for Children'. As with the Education Reform Bill in the middle to late 1980s, the Children Act is about children, not for them or belonging to them, and therefore there is little opportunity for them to influence the way it is applied to them, especially in the context of schooling provision.

2.25 Young people are not knowledgeable about key elements of equality legislation, or about education legislation and guidance such as Circular 10/99, which deals with schools' powers to exclude children and gives guidance on good practice in keeping students in school rather than excluding them either for a fixed term or permanently. Yet, there is no evidence of them being encouraged and empowered to use such legislation and guidance to inform themselves, safeguard their interests, own up to their responsibilities and defend their rights.

2.26 Government continues to treat them as if they fall into two camps: conformist, going with the flow, politically disinterested and consensually ignorant; or feral, anti-social, feckless, terrorist or jihadist. The introduction of and increasing use of anti-social behaviour orders in recent times, the disproportionate levels of 'stop and search' among particular ethnic groups in the 'war against terror' and the growing tendency to reach for legislation to curb young people's behaviour and tackle the involvement of a minority of them in street violence are worrying examples of Government's approach to young people who find themselves at odds with their community and with society.

2.27 The charter is geared to assist school students and parents in challenging the accepted form of governance by schools and politicians alike, i.e., ensuring coercive compliance by the application of endless laws and ruling over a school and parent population ill informed about children's human rights and schools' accountability to their learning community and for complying with legislation; a school and parent population that is given incomplete information, out of time and out of context.

2.28 The discussions I have had with school students and their families suggest that they want politicians and schools to acknowledge that while standards have undoubtedly improved, the debate about school improvement, school effectiveness and raising attainment has largely passed children by, except insofar as schools place greater demands on them in terms of behaviour and discipline, application to their studies, tests and examinations, etc.

2.29 Few politicians and social commentators note the fact that it is precisely in that period of educational 'improvement' that we have seen the greatest number of children out of school and the largest number of young people from one single ethnic group dying at the hands of one another, year on year.

2.30 Academies and the 'Building Schools for the Future' programme are not having any visible impact on that process of systematizing social exclusion among the young. In fact, it could be argued that they are adding massively to the problem in that, despite new, spacious and well appointed buildings and a vast improvement in the learning environment, many are still excluding children and are failing to ensure that Every Child Matters enough to be given their educational entitlement having regard to their educational and emotional support needs.

2.31 It costs the government roughly £100,000 to keep one young person in prison for a year. For every ten young people in a young offender institution, the cost is £1m. Where those young people are looked after children in local authority care, the cumulative cost is considerably higher.

2.32 How much more cheaply and in a more humane and children friendly environment could the state provide for such people, before they offend, in a learning environment that acknowledges their emotional and developmental support needs, rather than one that effectively makes them yet one more statistic among the 135,000 children of compulsory school age who are not in mainstream schooling or, worse still, the 85,000 prisoners in the nation's prisons.

2.33 If we genuinely believe that 'one size does not fit all' and that you don't treat people equally by treating them all the same, why can't we fix the regime of schooling such that it caters for the diverse needs of an increasingly diverse learning community, including teachers as learners? If we are 'building schools for the future', why can't we build Learning Campuses that are inclusive of all children (those with severe learning difficulties should receive the support and adjustments that would enable them to be included) and sustain vibrant communities of learning, where teachers and other professionals could cater for all learners according to need?

2.34 There is now enough evidence, for example, that where there is a focus on the needs of students who resist or are excluded from school, as in alternative learning environments such as supplementary schools, and community based alternative education provision, those students flourish and regain a zest for learning. In such provision, the more they succeed, having been encouraged by mainstream schooling to write themselves off as failures, is the more confident and ambitious they become. It is precisely this form of provision that the government is now trying to knock into shape through its 'Back on Track' *programme*. And, it is precisely that type of learning environment and approach to pedagogy many colleges are seeking to provide for the 14-19 year olds who might otherwise be 'not in education, employment or training'.

2.35 Side by side with the rise in the number of school age children that now make up that 135,000, the last decade has seen the steady expansion of police presence in schools. Whereas before schools maintained a close liaison with the police and encouraged them to be involved in supporting the curriculum in respect of matters to do with the role of the police in the community, road safety, personal safety, avoiding the risk of offending and the consequences of drug and alcohol abuse, many schools, secondary in particular, now have a mini police station. A report in the *Southend Evening Echo,* 18 June 2008, said of the police presence in Shoeburyness High School:

> *Headteachers decide on suspensions and expulsions but the officers can look to make arrests should an incident warrant their intervention. Headteacher Sue Murphy said she would recommend every school have an officer based on site to deal with issues, help educate pupils and make everyone feel safer.*

2.36 So, you walk into some schools and before you see an office marked 'Home/School Liaison', 'Parent and Pupil Support' or 'Parent Partnership', you come face to face with the mini-police station staffed by uniformed police officers. Sometimes, you are met at the inner entrance to the school by such officers.

2.37 This fails to take account of the historical relationship between the police and black and white working class communities in Britain. It fails to acknowledge that many parents of today's school and college students were themselves victims of, and had their life chances compromised by, the operation of the 'Sus' laws in the late 1970s and throughout the 1980s. It fails to acknowledge that while today's police officers might be befriending them and supposedly acting in a learning support capacity in school, other police officers could well be repeatedly making them targets of 'Stop and Search'.

2.38 Police are now routinely intervening in incidents in schools that are properly the responsibility of school managers to deal with. Students are carted off to police stations in police vehicles to be dealt with either by way of a ticking off, a caution, or charges for a range of indictable offences, often before parents are informed of their involvement in any incident. Children are therefore finding themselves put on the national DNA database even when the police have no cause to proceed against them.

2.39 'DNA samples can be taken by the police from anyone arrested and detained in custody in connection with a recordable offence'. (Home Affairs Committee report, 2007). Baroness Scotland (now Attorney General) confirmed in her evidence to that committee that 'three quarters of the young black male population will soon be on the DNA database'.

2.40 For many children and parents in urban areas, schooling is conducted as if against a backcloth of youth offending. It presupposes a youth offending culture that the school must at all costs keep far from its gates. When young people display behaviours that the school sees as manifestations of that culture, it employs a 'zero tolerance' approach which inexorably leads to fixed period if not permanent exclusions, typically of black and ethnic minority and dual heritage students.

2.41 The school compartmentalizes support for children's moral, social, emotional, spiritual and academic development into subjects that are taught: Personal, Social, Health Education, and Citizenship, Religious Education, Community Cohesion, and the National Curriculum. Support for children in unlearning the behaviours that characterize how they are in their peer groups, in their community or sometimes in their homes, too often takes the form of dealing with the way they conform, or not, to a set of rules: 'You do this... You don't do that'. And too often we are told that teachers are far too busy 'to do all that other stuff'.

2.42 But, doing 'all that other stuff' is something for which, increasingly, parents are finding ways of acting collectively to devise methods and to give support to one another, as is illustrated in Attachment 3.

2.43 Whether in relation to managing discipline in schools or dealing with youth offending, Britain adopts a more punitive approach to young people of school age than most other European countries. It certainly excludes more children from school than any other European country. Such punitive measures, however, have the effect of compounding young people's social exclusion and sense of being rejected by society, rather than 'teaching them a lesson' that might deter them and others from similar conduct. Some 84% of young people reoffend within three months of release from young offender institutions.

2.44 There remains a strong correlation between social inequality, schooling outcomes, and social exclusion. For example, despite the overall improvement in GCSE results annually in the last decade, the gap between the results for black Caribbean students, boys in particular, and boys from other ethnic groups shows no signs of narrowing:

5 A* – C	2005	2006	2007	2008
White boys	38.9	40.4	41.9	44.2
Mixed (W/BC)	25.8	27.5	27.5	33.9
Black Caribbean	**21.2**	**22.7**	**26.5**	**29.5**
Black African	29.7	31.7	34.7	36.9
Indian	52.4	54.3	56.3	60.1
Chinese	62.8	59.7	66.3	63.6

While the picture for black Caribbean girls is marginally better, they remain the worst performing group when compared with girls from other ethnic groups, including whites:

5 A* – C	2005	2006	2007	2008
White girls	47.0	48.4	49.8	52.0
Mixed (W/BC)	34.8	37.4	39.6	41.7
Black Caribbean	**32.5**	**36.0**	**38.5**	**42.1**
Black African	39.8	43.3	45.6	49.5
Indian	62.8	64.3	67.2	69.9
Chinese	75.2	72.2	74.0	75.4

2.45 Black boys are:
- three times more likely to be excluded from school than their white counterparts
- ten times more likely to be the subject of 'managed moves' (voluntary withdrawal by parents , usually at the instigation of the school)
- six to eight times more likely to be stopped and searched
- six to eight times more likely to be arrested than whites
- 2.7% of population aged 10-17 but 8.5% of all those arrested in that age group in England & Wales (Home Affairs Committee, 2007)

2.46 As early as 1969, the first all-party parliamentary select committee on race relations and immigration published their report *The Problem of Coloured School Leavers* in which they claimed that:

West Indian parents have unrealistic aspirations for their children.

One problem they identified was that West Indian parents equate length of time spent in school with quality of educational outcomes.

The source of their high aspirations was principally their life experience with Britain in the Caribbean and *that*, 'underdeveloped' though it was, they had seen ample evidence in the Caribbean of education as a route to self improvement and social transformation, especially for the children of the poor and dispossessed.

2.47 Since the late 1960s, even as the children of Caribbean immigrants made Britain their home and tried to accommodate to the British schooling system, the teaching profession was treated to a range of theories of 'race' and intelligence:

- Hans Eysenck & Arthur Jensen – 1969/73
- Charles Murray & the Bell Curve – 1990s
- Phillipe Rushton – 1990s
- James Watson – 2007

2.48   The basic thesis of all those proponents of theories of scientific racism is that higher scores of whites relative to blacks in aptitude tests are explained by genetically determined differences in intelligence and ability. These theories, especially of Eysenck and Jensen, had a huge influence upon those training teachers and educational psychologists as well as those devising intelligence tests. Not surprisingly, therefore, such tests were racially and culturally biased to the extent that when applied to black children they resulted in an excessive number of them being judged to be 'educationally subnormal' (ESN). These theories, and the practices that flowed from them led the Caribbean Education and Community Workers Association in 1970 to convene a conference to discuss the ESN issue. That conference led to the publication of Bernard Coard's seminal work, *How the West Indian Child is Made Educationally Subnormal in the British School System.*

The process by which scientific racism influenced education theory, teacher education and pedagogy, and laid a platform of low expectations as far as the performance and achievement of black children were concerned, had its parallel in the way eugenics impacted upon education theory and practice with regard to disabled people. This gave rise to special schools and the belief that children with moderate to severe learning difficulties needed to be segregated and placed in 'special schools'.

2.49   Almost four decades later, researchers are finding that teachers' assessment of black students fails to reflect their performance in public examinations and that those students are being marked down by teachers as a result of stereotyping and low expectations, a phenomenon that was not evident in their assessment of Chinese and Indian students.
<http://www.guardian.co.uk/education/2010/apr/04/sats-marking-race-stereotypes>

2.50 Black Caribbean students have bumped along the bottom of the school examination charts since the Select Committee reported in 1969, despite a number of government initiatives from Section 11 funding (Local Gov't Act 1966) to 'Ethnic Minority Achievement Grants' to projects for 'Raising the Achievement of Black Caribbean Boys'.

2.51 Analysing the 1991 and 2001 Census results, Simpson et al reported:

> the **net disadvantage** of ethnic minorities in the labour market has become greater for men born in the UK. Those born in the UK have gained higher qualifications than their overseas-born parents, but the playing field has become more uneven. This ethnic penalty means greater unemployment for Indian, Pakistani, Bangladeshi and Caribbean men, and even more so for those born in the UK
>
> L. Simpson, K. Purdam, A. Tajar, E. Fieldhouse, V. Gavalas, M. Tranmer, J. Pritchard and D. Dorling, *Ethnic minority populations and the labour market: an analysis of the 1991 and 2001 Census* DWP, 2006

2.52 In Bristol in 2007, I worked with 80 black 12-16 year old school students, two thirds of whom were boys, from three schools including an Academy. In the course of the day, I set them the following task:

At this stage of your life, write down the three things you fear most.
Their deepest fears, presented here on the basis of the frequency with which they appeared were:
- Dying
- Death
- Being killed/murdered
- Going pen (going to prison)
- Getting stabbed
- My loved ones dying around me
- Anything happening to my family
- Losing loved ones
- **Our youths**
- Not achieving goals
- Not being able to afford the things I want in the future(house,

car, etc)
- Not getting the opportunities I want
- Not succeeding
- Living by myself
- The Tories in power

2.53 When I asked the entire group to describe what their schools did to engage with them in dealing with those fears, they could point to not one intervention save for the guidance and support a few individuals and their families were receiving from teachers who were 'safe' and with whom they had developed a good relationship. Indeed, the majority of the students stated that their schools did not know they harboured these fears as 'it's not the kind of thing the school is interested in'.

2.54 An equally important and instructive exercise was to discuss among themselves the following question:

Why is it that some young people (boys **and** girls) from the same family do well at school, live peaceably with their peers and manage themselves well in their community, while their siblings do the complete opposite and ... end up dead?

The students identified a range of key issues:
- Self esteem
- Level of aspirations
- Capacity to resist peer pressure
- Making fast money
- Reasons for and consequences of resisting parental guidance and discipline
- Self management skills
- Society's expectations that black boys can't do well
- Quality of support from people they respect, including some teachers
- Not wanting to be seen as a 'goodie two shoes'
- 'My brother is a geek. He so would never survive on road'
- 'Need to be tough and deal with mans that disrespect you'
- 'You have to be able to handle yourself on road'

2.55 In this latter section, I have concentrated on one group of school students. I make no apology for that because as the statistics show, black Caribbean and mixed (white and black Caribbean) students continue to be the lowest achievers in the school system. Pakistani and Bangladeshi students and white students in urban or rural areas will have a possibly similar list of issues that arise within their peer groups, in their communities, in their homes, in their schooling experience and in the way society sees them.

2.56 All of those issues, irrespective of the ethnicity of the students, are ones with which schools should concern themselves, especially if they profess to be working in the interests of children and in partnership with parents to support children's learning and social, moral, emotional, spiritual and cultural development. Sadly, however, 'partnership' is often interpreted to mean parents working to an agenda set by the school and with methods and arrangements that best suit the school, including the timing of meetings with the school. Partnership is seldom the two way process the term implies.

2.57 What is more, schools show no signs of appreciating the power imbalance that is built into those partnership arrangements. There is a huge imbalance in the knowledge the school possesses, e.g., about policies and procedures, especially those relating to exclusion, streaming and setting, special needs, and schools' powers generally, than that which most parents have. Parents are not expected to set the agenda for discussion of matters to do with their children, based upon the issues which they are seeking to assist their children in addressing, and that might have an impact on the quality of their performance in school, both academically and socially.

2.58 Many schools do not credit the work parents do individually and collectively in their homes and in their communities to support their children and assist them with strategies for managing themselves in school, peer group and community (see Attachment 3). If parents are not encouraged to see those as matters which could form their agenda for working in partnership with schools, then for many of them the notion of 'partnership' remains one-sided if not totally vacuous.

2.59 Parents are not a homogenous group any more than children are. The stubborn fact remains, however, that schools demonstrate 'attitude' to some parents while, in their dealings with others, there is a mutual presumption of respect. It is for this reason that there needs to be a definition of the rights and responsibilities of schools, teachers, students and parents, as we did in *Born to be Great: A Charter on Promoting the Achievement of Black Caribbean Boys* which I produced with the National Union of Teachers (NUT) in 2007.

2.60 In January 2009, the NUT published a companion policy document *Opening Locked Doors: Educational Achievement and White Working Class YoungPeople*, highlighting social class as 'the most neglected and powerful influence on children's achievement'. Christine Blower, General Secretary of the National Union of Teachers, the largest teachers' union, stated that:

> *Social class has the greatest effect on educational achievement. It is still the case that how much your parents earn and the quality of their own education has the greatest influence on the achievement of their children ... The Government's job is to tackle disadvantage and despair by offering practical and effective proposals to give hope to parents and their children in these communities. The NUT agrees with John Denham when he says that disadvantages caused by social class and racism need to be tackled both together.*

2.61 Social class and racism not only have a powerful influence on children's achievement, they also help to define the contours of the relationship between schools and certain groups of parents and the nature of the 'partnership' they seek to forge with those parents.

2.62 Government could and should decide to be proactive in rebalancing power between schools and parents by:
- acknowledging the work that parents and young people do in communities (in parent support groups, in supplementary schools, in voluntary education projects, in family learning sets) and funding such work appropriately
- requiring schools to take account of such work and of the community's educational aspirations when planning how to work with parents and communities in support of children's learning and development

2.63 Most parents have as great an abhorrence of the culture of 'road' and of the aggression and violence visited upon one another by young people, whether acting as individuals, in groups or in gangs as schools do. Many parents struggle to make the influence of the home more powerful than that of the peer group or of 'road'. They, like the school, have to deal with the age old manifestations of adolescent behaviour among 11–18 year olds.

2.64 As one RC primary school student wrote in answer to a test question:

> The greatest miricle [sic] in the Bible is when Joshua told his son to stand still and he obeyed him.

2.65 A 13 year old student was excluded for five days for saying what he genuinely believed was a more appropriate grace before meals. Everyone else said daily: 'For what we are about to receive may the Lord make us truly thankful'. He, however, decided that the school meals were so exceptionally bad that it was more fitting to ask for a different favour from the Lord and so he said, alas too loudly: 'From what we are about to receive may the good Lord deliver us'. He and his family protested against the exclusion on the grounds that they at home and the school encouraged the boy to speak the truth. It was therefore unjust to punish him when he spoke the truth to God.

2.66 Unlike schools, parents cannot operate a 'zero tolerance' policy and permanently exclude their children. Many parents find it difficult to build the kind of relationship with the school where they could share the challenges they are facing, the strategies they are applying in dealing with them and their ideas of how the school can work together with them to support the child through whatever period of challenge or crisis they might be experiencing.

2.67 Instead, it is more usual for parents to be summoned to the school to be told: that their child is sailing dangerously close to the exclusion wind, or, why their child is being temporarily or permanently excluded.

2.68 Some headteachers argue that the raising achievement and school effectiveness agenda places such pressure on teachers that working with parents in those ways is well nigh impossible. Schooling, therefore, is more and more about preparing for public examinations and children demonstrating that they can earn themselves and the school high grades. Parent agreements and school/parent partnerships are therefore increasingly geared towards ensuring that students display the right attitudes and dispositions to bring about those outcomes, rather than supporting young people's rounded development as social beings needing help in acquiring, applying and embedding the values and skills that make them fit for living in civil society as active citizens.

2.69   A schooling system built upon the latter principles and operating with these goals will continue to generate planned and structured human obsolescence and social exclusion on the axis of class and of race and of gender.

2.70   The greatest indictment of the schooling system, no less than of the mass media, is that opportunities are not created for young people to debate and plan around these issues. They continue to be provided for and done unto, more often than not in spite of themselves.

2.71   School students themselves need to rescue schooling and reclaim education not only because it is a task too important to be left to politicians and to parents beguiled by the neo-liberal agenda, but because they have a responsibility to work together to determine the kind of schooling system that would help them make the future they face the future they actually want for themselves and their children in an increasingly globalized world and fractured society where social exclusion continues to mirror social injustice.

2.72   We need a Learner's Charter to provide a framework for them to do just that, unimpeded by the systems, structures and practices that constitute schooling today. When one looks at the pronouncements of the major political parties with respect to education, school students clearly cannot look to them to deliver empowerment and democratic participation any time soon.

That is why we need a Learner's Charter.

It is envisaged that a succinct Learner's Charter will be constructed on the basis of the following:

I Am

- I Am: Somebody
- I Am: Special
- I Am: Capable of striving to be whatever I want to be
- I Am: A person with high ambitions for myself
- I Am: Committed to applying myself so I can achieve my ambitions
- I Am: Expecting to see evidence at all times that, as I apply myself, my teachers, my parents and the adults in my life have high ambitions for me also, and teach, support and guide me in a manner that enables me to realize my ambitions
- I Am: Capable of learning from my mistakes
- I Am: Capable of being a role model for my peers
- I Am: Capable of learning from the example of others

I Am Not

- I Am Not: Worthless
- I Am Not: Ugly
- I Am Not: A sexual object
- I Am Not: My designer label.
- I Am Not: My Ipod.
- I Am Not: My postcode.
- I Am Not: My peer group profile.
- I Am Not: My facebook profile.
- I Am Not: My gang membership.
- I Am Not: Too mean to assist others
- I Am Not: Too proud to ask for help
- I Am Not: A failure.

I have rights

- I have the right to know my rights and responsibilities and to exercise them
- A basic right I have is the right to know where I came from and how I came to be here
- I have the right to know how well or how badly I am

performing as a learner and as a member of the learning community

- I have a right to fair and just treatment by my teachers and peers
- I have a right to be listened to and to have my views taken into account
- I have a right to comment, constructively, upon the quality of teaching and the quality of my learning as a result of the teaching I receive
- I have a right to be assisted in discovering how I learn best and a duty to communicate that knowledge to others
- I have a duty to take responsibility for my own learning and to apply myself in such a manner as to be capable of reaching my goals
- I have a right not to be discriminated against or disadvantaged on account of the language I speak at home, but to have that language respected and used to support my learning of other languages
- I believe that opportunities should be created for more formal conversations between teachers and students about:
  a. how students are learning
  b. teachers' expectations of students and the impact of those expectations on the quality of their teaching and on their assessment of students' work and overall performance
  c. how students experience their teaching
  d. the culture of the learning community and its impact on students' wellbeing

I have responsibilities

- I have responsibilities to myself, to my family and to society
- I have a responsibility to the learning community of which I am a part
- I have a duty to take responsibility for my own learning and to apply myself in such a manner as to be capable of reaching my goals and to seek help and support when I feel I need it
- I have a duty to take responsibility for my own behaviour and for how it impacts on others
- I have a personal responsibility to conduct myself in a manner that helps to make the school a place where all can feel valued

and can learn and teach in safety and comfort
- I have a responsibility to know how the rights I now enjoy as a citizen were won and to safeguard them

I have beliefs and values
- I believe that if I don't care where I am going, any road would get me there and sometimes that 'road' leads to prison or the grave
- I believe that my parents and family, my teachers, peers and the adults in my life can help me find my strengths and build upon them
- I believe in the dignity and worth of every human being
- I have respect for life, both mine and everyone else's
- I believe that everyone has a right to live
- I believe that everyone has a right to live with respect and dignity
- I believe that everyone has a right to work, study, and enjoy their leisure in an environment in which that right is respected
- I believe that respect for oneself and for others grows by giving it practical expression in all aspects of daily living
- I believe that this means I should confront oppression on the grounds of 'race', gender, class, disability, sexual orientation, age, faith/religion, where people live, how they live their lives, how they look, how they dress, or their educational attainment
- I believe that I should safeguard the weak and defenceless from exploitation as a matter of duty and civic responsibility
- I believe that I must take responsibility for ensuring that I do not make people suffer or deny them their rights on account of any of the above grounds
- I believe in the human rights of all people and am committed to upholding those rights in all aspects of my dealings with the public
- I believe it is a fundamental human right to be able to go about my daily business without being called names or attacked physically because of the colour of my skin, or any other aspect of my identity
- I believe it is a fundamental human right to be able to go about my lawful business anywhere in this city or country, without fear of being attacked for not belonging to that place or to any

group in that place
- I believe that combating inequality and discrimination is part of the practice of building a human rights culture, a culture that upholds respect for the dignity and worth of every person
- I believe that each person must be encouraged to see themselves as enjoying the rights and civil liberties that were won through the struggles of those who went before us:
    Struggles against chattel slavery
    Struggles against child labour
    Struggles against the 'colour bar' and apartheid in the provision of goods and services
    Struggles against unfair dismissal
    Struggles against bullying and intimidation in the workplace
    Struggles against domestic violence
    Struggles against the physical and sexual abuse of children
    Struggles against child poverty
    Struggles against homelessness
    Struggles for the right to vote
    Struggles for a living wage
    Struggles for equal pay for equal work
    Struggles for gender equality, disability equality and race equality
    Struggles for equal access to education and employment
    Struggles for Health & Safety at work
    Struggles for the right to form trade unions
    Struggles for humane working conditions
- I believe, therefore, that I have a democratic responsibility to safeguard hard-won rights, work to extend civil rights, protect the environment and act as an agent of change
- I believe that I am part of a multiethnic, multifaith, multilingual, multicultural and multiclass society and that inequality is as much part of the diversity of the society as is 'race', gender, etc.
- I believe that *I am the future* of this society and that the society belongs to me as much as it does to everybody else
- I believe that I have as much right as anybody else to determine the kind of society I want it to be; I do not believe that I forfeit or pass up that right when I cast my vote at specified intervals; I claim that right and with it the responsibility to work with

others and make sure that the future we face is the future we actually want for ourselves and future generations

- I believe that as school students we can best learn about democracy by making the process of schooling itself more democratic and involving learners more routinely in consultation and in decision making
- I believe that empowering the individual to develop his/her capacity to act in a self-directing way and to take collective action with others in pursuit of change is at the very heart of the process of managing and expanding a democratic culture
- I believe that my school, my home and the community in which I live could assist my development by learning from the role of 'the Village' in traditional societies where:
  - the whole village takes responsibility for guiding the child to adopt and share the values that define the community and regulate the conduct of young and old alike
  - in so doing, it encourages the child to develop a sense of moral purpose and to see the community's code of conduct as having the same moral force as the law of the land
  - in other words, the child learns to act with 'moral purpose' and to develop their own sense of right and wrong
  - as the child grows, the village helps them to develop and sustain a sense of wellbeing and to be an effective and well adjusted member of the community
- In the absence of 'the village', home, school and my own peer group could assist my development by attending to 'critical factors in constructive Self-building' as indicated in the 'SELF' diagram
- I believe that these factors are essential to my wellbeing
- I believe that they help to promote 'living values' and the development of insight and emotional literacy, and to discourage amoral conduct and antisocial behaviour.

'The Village'

In traditional societies, 'Rites of Passage' are part of a process by which a whole village, and not just 'family' (blood relatives), take responsibility for bringing up children

Just by allowing children to be normal and guiding them to adopt socially acceptable attitudes and sound values, the village assists the child in developing the holistic self

The whole village takes responsibility for guiding the child to adopt and share the values that define the community and regulate the conduct of young and old alike

In so doing, it encourages the child to develop a sense of *moral purpose* and to see the community's code of conduct as having the same moral force as the law of the land

The child thus learns to do things because they are regarded by those around them as right and proper

The child learns to act with 'moral purpose' and to develop their own sense of right and wrong

S/he learns what would invite the disapproval or wrath of adults in the community, irrespective of whether or not they are relatives or family friends

Without ever using the word 'values' or talking about 'the holistic self', the village community helps and guides the child in her/his self development

As the child grows, the village helps them to develop and sustain a sense of wellbeing and to be an effective and well adjusted member of the community

Self knowledge, positive self esteem, a sense of self worth, the capacity to manage oneself, having the self discipline to endure temporary pain for longer term gain, all help create and sustain a sense of well being

In the absence of 'the village', home and school must attend to 'Critical Factors in Constructive Self-building' as indicated in the 'SELF' diagram (Attachment 2)

This is especially necessary for all underachieving students, and those labelled and socially excluded for whatever reasons, social class, economic, cultural, ethnic or religious background, sexuality, physique, etc.

Foundations of Individualized Learning & Personal Development

Family Centred Approaches to Youth Conflict
Manchester, March 2004

[Extracts from *Taking A Stand – Gus John Speaks on education, race, social action and civil unrest 1980-2005*, Gus John Partnership, Manchester, pp.143-64]

We, as facilitators of children's learning and self development, must be seen to model by our own conduct and by living our values, the behaviours and principles we wish to see our children exhibit.

These sessions have been planned in conjunction with young people and their parents to whom I have been giving support, during the last six months, in developing strategies for resolving conflict. They have also been informed by my discussions with learning mentors working in secondary schools.

The conflict situations that have caused pain and distress to whole families, and that have involved the police and the Court system on occasions, include:

- Parents being banned from entering school premises because of physical aggression towards teachers over schools' treatment of their children;
- young people's revenge attacks upon one another;
- verbal aggression, escalating to physical violence, in and around their schools and in the community;
- physical aggression by young people against their mothers;
- parents and other family members at war with one another over incidents involving physical harm to their children.

The issues that have been identified in the sessions we have had so far include the following, as reported by parents and young people:

- Some parents gave examples of the efforts they had made to work in partnership with schools, including telephoning the school on a regular basis to enquire about their children's progress, or to inform the school about events in the family which they felt might have a bearing on the child's mood and conduct. In spite of those efforts and the relationship the parents felt they had formed with teachers, children would be given fixed term exclusions without the parents being alerted that anything was wrong at school, or that the school was about to send the child home.

- African-Caribbean boys, as young as 10, were being bullied and harassed by older boys to join gangs and to tell a web of lies to their parents about their whereabouts. When their parents went to complain to the parents of gang members, they were met not just with denial but with hostility and aggression because those complaining were 'calling their children criminals'. Hostility developed because the relatives of the gang members started going about in the community saying nasty things about those who had complained about their children's conduct.
- Girls in school were in conflict with one another over boys, a not unusual occurrence. The conflict took on a more sinister dimension, however, because the black girls and boys were harassing those other black girls about how *black* they were. Girls were being viciously bullied for being 'too black' and 'too ugly'. If the latter were also very bright and hardworking, they were ostracized even further. That caused misery not only to the girls themselves but to their families. When parents and other siblings saw those girls becoming more and more miserable, unable to sleep, demotivated and hating the very idea of going to school or college, they decided to take action. That resulted in confrontation with the ringleaders of those bullies and the opposing sides getting their 'posse' involved, thus prolonging the conflict.
- Mothers complained about being 'manhandled' and physically assaulted by their sons, either because of the mother's protest at the boy's treatment of his sister or because of the mother's insistence that he should not come and go as he liked, sometimes not coming home and not saying where he was or who he was with.
- Other mothers were distressed about conflicts between them and their sons as a result of forming a relation with a new partner, typically after many years of bringing up children on their own. They felt they were being bullied by their sons into choosing between them and the new man in their life.
- Young people complained about not being listened to by parents and teachers, and therefore 'giving up' on trying to share what's going on for them. For them, this had serious consequences when conflicts arose between their parents, typically mothers, and their school, or between them and their peers.

One thing all participants agreed upon, however, was that nursing conflicts was hard work and an obstacle to progress and meaningful living.

The other thing that was generally accepted by all was that 'we heap as much misery upon one another as the system piles upon us', and therefore, we have to devise methods within our own communities for sorting out problems, avoiding conflict and building peace. We all had to take responsibility for that, because every young bully comes from a home, often with very protective parents, however much those parents might themselves be indulging in bullying behaviour.

Parents talked passionately and at length about how much more difficult we make it for our children by not providing them with the skills to manage themselves in school and in the face of the pressures facing them in the community. Some parents readily admitted to being too stressed, 'too busy trying to make ends meet' to even know how to prepare their sons to handle what they're facing out there in school and in the community around them. Those parents paid tribute to those learning mentors, black and white, who were plainly very committed to helping their children do well, in whom those children confided, and who made a point of visiting them at home to discuss how they as parents could support their children better, and help them make schooling a more positive and productive experience.

A theme which everyone kept returning to, therefore, was the need for us to find ways of supporting one another within our communities, sharing one another's burdens and taking collective responsibility for the development and safeguarding of our children.

Arising out of those discussions, therefore, I have summarized the things we said we would deal with in these sessions, as follows:

Parents as their children's teachers

We agreed that we teach our children from birth and that, for better or for worse, they learn and pattern themselves more upon what they experience at home than what they are taught in school. We agreed that schools are not natural units of social organization and that many children find them quite frightening and alienating places.

Since we are so crucial in our children's development of a sense of what is right and wrong, what is acceptable and not so desirable conduct, we, as facilitators of children's learning and self development, must be seen to model by our own conduct and by living our values, the behaviours and principles we wish to see our children exhibit.

But that means we need to be clear about our own values, where they come from, and how we express them in our dealings with our children and with all others with whom they see us interacting.

Some parents spoke about the way they saw their children changing before their very eyes because of how they saw them being treated by their partners. A number of women said that, as a result, they made a decision to throw out their partners, even though they knew it would cause those partners' biological children some heartache.

Talking and Encouraging Children to Talk

We agreed our 'Number One Priority' was to have a session on 'talking':

- Encouraging children to speak and to share by showing them we are keen to know what's happening for them and that we are *listening*
- Valuing their point of view
- Encouraging their friends, with whom they typically share so much, to get to know the attitudes we have to our child's upbringing and the values we seek to have her/him develop
- Demonstrating that we could disagree with them without being judgemental
- Encouraging them at all things to consider how they might have handled any given situation differently
- Encouraging them to weigh up the benefits or disadvantages of their different responses and the values that are reflected in their choice of response
- Assisting them in de-coding their schooling experience and in developing strategies for surviving schooling
- Being honest with them and owning up to not having the knowledge or experience to deal with any particular situation
- Understanding that if children see us being upfront about our need for help and more informed guidance, they would themselves see it as normal to seek help and not believe they could always sort things out for themselves
- Encouraging positive relationships between our children and

significant others in their lives so that we know there are reliable people they feel comfortable about going to, even if, for whatever reason, they feel awkward about coming to us with the heavy stuff We have agreed to explore those ten issues further in the session after this, which will be devoted exclusively to considering the value of 'talk', and how to encourage it and create space for it.

We will devote the third session to looking at 'International Human Rights Standards' governing the rights of children, namely:
- The best interests of the child must be paramount (Article 3)
- Children have a right to be heard (A.12)
- Children have a right not to be discriminated against on the basis of, for example, class, race, ethnicity, religion/faith or gender (A.2)
- And we could add, 'OR because of the failings of either parent'.

We would relate this to the way children are treated in our homes, in school, in the community and by providers of public services. We would look at the implications of that for the attitudes children adopt towards one another, towards what they share with us, in their interactions with teachers, towards resolving conflict and in relating to fairness and justice. We would also examine how we can ensure our children are not discriminated against or exploited.

Children also have a right to guidance and support in developing the positive and holistic SELF.

We discussed this briefly in an earlier session and agreed to return to it over a couple of further sessions. We agreed that in doing so, we would explore a range of 'Factors in Constructive Self-building' and we would prepare for that session by reflecting upon the following and bringing our suggestions as to how we relate to each of them and could support our children in developing them. The notes that follow are meant to stimulate discussion and to assist each participant in identifying factors that have worked for them.

Factors such as:-
Positive identification with those that look like you
Positive attitude to your own body and all your characteristic features
Positive acknowledgement of your roots

Positive feedback about how you are and about what you do

- We know how much it matters to us to be told how well or how badly we are doing? How can we give encouragement to one another and to our children? How can we encourage them to be more positive towards one another and their achievements, and not feel that they should automatically display attitudes of hostility and resentment towards one another? How can we show more evidence of joy and celebration at one another's achievements and not give expression to the belief that 'we can't bear to see one another prosper'?

Positive examples of how you should be and how you should act

- How can we, by living our values, sharing one another's burdens, taking individual responsibility for our own conduct and acting collectively to support our youth and build our communities, provide examples to our young people as to how they should be and how they should act?

Being listened to and having your point of view taken seriously, especially when you are hurting and crying out for help

- How can we encourage active listening and 'emotional listening' in our homes and in our interactions with one another, so that we don't have to suffer in silence and our partners, children, relatives, friends or work colleagues don't take us for granted?

Identification of personality traits and character

- How well do we know ourselves and what we are like, the kind of 'character' we have? How well do we assist our children in identifying their own personality traits and building sound character?

Acknowledgment of what you are predisposed to do because of them

- You come to know that by being conscious of yourself but also by what others tell you about how they experience you. Therefore, learning to nurture and cultivate some of those traits and to bring others under control
- That's about sifting the ones that are conducive to personal development and growth from those that could obstruct your progress and make you socially abhorrent in the eyes of others

Capacity to make mistakes and not be defeated by them

- This means being prepared to take risks and to accept that 'to err is human', however much of a perfectionist you consider yourself to be.

Learning that no one fails once they've genuinely done their best, but that that 'best' could be built upon and made even better

- If we develop that positive attitude towards our own performance, on whatever front, we encourage those around us to strive to be the best by acknowledging their individual effort and hard work. This is especially important in giving support and feedback to our children. If we look only at the mark they are given and compare it with that of their siblings or their friends, we could discourage them hugely but not acknowledging the progress they made and the fact that they may have surpassed the target they set against themselves. Their siblings or friends may have a higher mark but failed to move an inch.

Capacity to see what went wrong and learn from mistakes

- It is one thing to make mistakes and not be defeated by them, it is quite another to keep repeating them and failing to learn any lessons from them. It is by putting ourselves through the discipline of self scrutiny and being honest about what it is that causes us to choose the same path over and over again, that we are able to change course. enable our children, friends and others in our lives to learn from our situation, and guide them on the basis of our experience.

Capacity to develop a sense of humour

- Do we take ourselves too seriously? Do we react in ways which encourage our children to see every disappointment as a cause of deep frustration and every joke as being at their expense?
- If we have a tendency to be uptight and ready to take on the world, we invite or search out conflict. Anyone unfortunate enough to step on our toe could well be risking 'life and limb'. It also prevents us from seeing adversity as the imposter that he is.

Capacity to show compassion

- That is about expressing our basic humanity and having the ability to reach out to others in situations which would test us similarly, were we to find ourselves in such situations. Here, again, this is about living our values and giving example to our young people about the importance of being able to attach value to others and treat them as they themselves would wish to be treated.

Capacity to understand other people's reality and not judge on the basis of your own

- What is that famous saying: Never judge a man until you have walked a mile in his moccasins? Adults and young people alike engage in various forms of bullying and destructive tittle-tattle by passing judgement on others on the basis of their own reality. How can we encourage children to see people for what they are and respect their realities, and not harass them directly or cause them damage by saying all sorts of hurtful and prejudiced things about them?

Capacity to express one's innermost feelings and not blame oneself for having those feelings

- That's a tricky one. Blocking off the space in which you or your children could express such feelings without being made to feel guilty about sharing them could be a form of oppression. Here, again, laying the foundations for talking and sharing in a safe and secure environment is critical. Too often, even people who live under the same roof pass each other every hour of the day like ships in the night. Relationships and interactions become contaminated and progress is possible only when individuals make the space to talk openly about the weight they are carrying.
- Why is it tricky? It depends on time, place and audience, and what feelings one feels impelled to express. We all have to accept responsibility for the effect that our conduct and what we say have on others. Our innermost feelings could be feelings of anger that are designed to hurt. They could also be feelings of hatred towards particular individuals and groups. Expressing innermost feelings of hatred of homosexuals, of disabled people or of Muslims, is clearly not the same as summoning up the courage to tell your

partner fifty reasons why he is a chauvinist pig.

Capacity to manage one's emotions
- How well do we manage our emotions, especially the more extreme ones? How do we manage loss, anger, frustration, ecstatic joy? How do we manage our emotions with sensitivity, having regard to the emotions of others around us and the possible impact of ours on them? What signals are we sending out to our children by the way we respond to their emotions, especially as they don't always take the temperature of ours before they boldly and sometimes demandingly express theirs? How we are assisting them in developing emotional literacy and handling their emotions in their interactions with others in a multiplicity of settings?

Having your confidence reinforced by your successes
- Like it was when you learnt to ride a bicycle. Or did you give up after the third tumble? Success breeds success. Remember what we said earlier about 'when you've done your best'. Your 'best' could always be built upon and the more you succeed, the more you have the confidence to take on new challenges.

Having your confidence reinforced by evidence of learning from your mistakes
- This was raised in a discussion about parenting and how parents encourage children to learn from their mistakes as parents. Making serious mistakes could often lead to a desire to 'shut down' completely. In relationships that go pear shaped, it sometimes leads to bitterness and a corrosive anger. The man or woman leaves, but you hang on to a load of emotional baggage ten times heavier than their body weight. And then, just when you think you are turning the corner and getting back in control of your own life, you hook up with someone who turns out to be not unlike the one before.

Capacity to accept praise
- Some people are very awkward about accepting praise, especially when they are not accustomed to being praised. We come to believe that 'we are not worth it', or 'I was only doing my duty', or 'I can't see what's so special about that'. Those reactions could easily

become an invitation to others to take you for granted, especially those around you for whom you do so very much daily. There are times when it is legitimate for you to say, to your children and your partner especially: 'I am glad you appreciate what I have done. I would see it as an even greater mark of appreciation if you tried to do the same more often'.

- We talked before about our children's tendency to 'diss' one another and be negative about how they look, how they dress, who they're with, and all sorts. We therefore need to be careful about our own behaviour, about what they see us do, how they see us react to others, how they hear us speak about others. If giving and accepting praise becomes the norm and they grow up with that from an early age, if that is reinforced by us as adults taking responsibility for how we speak about others and about their achievements, our children, more than likely, would go out there with more positive attitudes to themselves and others.

Capacity to accept other people receiving praise when you are not
- If we did the things we've just noted, it won't be so difficult in rejoice with others and help celebrate their achievements. It won't be so difficult to bask in their sunlight.

Capacity to give praise
- If we did those things, we, and especially our children, would learn to give praise more readily and more genuinely. How often do we hear some of our young people boast that they never say thanks for anything. One young person argued with me when I told him he had no manners, that: 'thanks belongs to God'. He was not too impressed when I told him: 'I am God, and if you cannot see and acknowledge me, then God doesn't want your thanks'. If we don't ensure that our children learn and are at ease with these values, we are encouraging their development as amoral people, without respect for themselves or for others.

Capacity to criticize in a sensitive manner
- Do we criticize in order to indulge ourselves and show off how smart we are, or do we criticize in order that the other person might learn, or might be encouraged to see things from a different

perspective? When we criticize in a destructive manner, we invite people to ignore the message and, rather, react to our anger, meanness, or whatever. They take on the messenger and miss the message. They feel the need to respond defensively and, sometimes, to restore their dignity which you stripped away by the manner of your criticism. Furthermore, we fail to allow space for the person to improve when we criticize in those ways. Again, the first place children see how such things are done, badly or well, is in the home and at our side as parents and carers. If our conduct isn't right, and if we celebrate our poor conduct and elevate it to a level of acceptability, that is what our children would see as appropriate in their dealings with us, and with others.

Capacity to respect yourself

- If we don't learn to respect ourselves, we cannot see the value in respecting others. Respecting one's SELF is about acknowledging that we are special and born to be great. We have a capacity for good and for evil. Since we have the capacity to nurture our potential for good as well as for evil, we have a corresponding duty to embrace values which make us fit for living in a civilized society. Respect is one such critical value.
- Some of us see, and encourage our children to see, having 'respect' as a sign of weakness. We encourage them to model our behaviour which, often, is a sign of a total lack of respect for ourselves and for those around us. That, however, does not stop us from demanding 'respect' from others. In other words, we don't show that we respect ourselves, but demand that others show us respect. This is a constant cause of aggravation in the family conflicts we deal with. Parents talk to children in the foulest of language and in the most aggressive manner, and then protest when those children talk to one another, and talk back to them, in the same manner and using the same language.
- That way of communicating then becomes the only one the children are comfortable with. They take it to every situation, especially in their interactions with their peers. Furthermore, those same parents would go mad with rage when schools exclude their children for persistent verbal abuse of teachers.

Capacity to respect others

- If we don't know how to respect ourselves and why we should, we would hardly see the point in showing respect to others, however respectful they are towards us. Some people who find our conduct disrespectful or unacceptable would remain silent and put it down to a lack of manners. Others might protest and not rise to our anger and abuse in reaction to their protest. Others would see us as wanting to be 'wrong and strong' and see it as their duty to cut us down to size, sometimes literally. 'Why did you shoot him?' Because 'He had no respect', or, 'He disrespected my woman'. 'To teach him some respect'. We have a generation of young people in our communities who are so much at ease with mindless, gratuitous, violence that it leads them to commit all kinds of barbaric acts in the name of 'respect', and yet, they have no 'respect' for life itself.
- Respect for oneself and for others grows by giving it expression in all aspects of daily living. Living without 'respect' dehumanizes us and renders us capable of barbarism.

Capacity to demand respect for yourself and safeguard your rights

- Each of us has a right to be treated with respect and dignity and a responsibility to treat others in a similar fashion in order that we could earn their respect.
- Some people choose to disrespect us and deny us our rights because of who we are, (poor people, gays and lesbians, women, or black people, unemployed and claiming benefit), or they think they have a right to do so because they see us as inferior to them. They do so more often than not without knowing the first thing about us and we, naturally, react out of a desire to uphold our dignity and assert that we have no intention of allowing ourselves to be treated in that manner. In doing so, we have anti-discrimination legislation to assist us.
- In relation to some of the issues highlighted at the beginning of this paper, however, how does our conduct measure up? Do we routinely show respect to one another in our homes and in our communities? How do we prevent our boys and men from engaging in various forms of gender subordination and disrespect of mothers, siblings, and other female members of the family? How

do we discourage those women and girls from putting up with it? What signals do we send out to our men that such conduct is unacceptable and would not be tolerated? How do we ensure that we are giving our boys the right messages about how to treat women, especially girlfriends and future female partners or wives?

Capacity to see disagreements as normal and healthy

- How do we have our disagreements about matters great and small, and make them constructive so that we move forward? Are we able to deal with them in a manner that does not result in aggravation and short or longer term conflict? Do we have the capacity to deal with matters and not let them fester? Do we have the capacity to set them aside once they have been dealt with, and not keep the embers burning so we could re-ignite them when it suits us?

Capacity to deal with conflict without resorting to verbal and physical violence

- How do we have our disagreements and retain respect for ourselves and for those with whom we are in conflict? How do we continue to give expression to that respect by taking responsibility for not allowing the disagreement to get out of hand, irrespective of what the other party to the conflict does? How do we take control of the situation and avoid verbal aggression, while at the same time putting our position across? How do we avoid being provoked to physical violence?

Capacity to make demands on oneself and meet the legitimate demands of others

- It is a natural tendency to do what we like best and put off, or avoid altogether, those things which we find less satisfying. How do we develop the capacity to set targets for ourselves to enable us to achieve our goals? How do we make changes in our routine and free up time for our self development; time to talk to our children, listen to them, and guide them in facing the many challenges confronting them; time to go to their school and talk about their progress; time to do the many things we keep postponing, while stressing ourselves out about not having done them? How do we build up sources of support so that we are not struggling with making those changes on our own? How do we encourage our children to not settle for the minimum, but to demand more of themselves? How do we assist them in developing the discipline necessary for their own progress, so that they could see the positive results of their efforts and of the sacrifices they make?

Capacity to hold one's own and demand one's rights

- How can we inform ourselves about our rights in order to be more confident about demanding them? How can we identify the responsibilities that we have so as to ensure that we do what is required of us, even as we make others accountable? How can we develop the capacity to be assertive with people, and in relation to systems and structures, that fail to respect our rights as parents, consumers, as citizens? How can we work collectively with others to make such people, systems and structures more responsive to our needs? How can we take our children through that same process so that they learn to be more socially responsible, socially competent and politically aware?

Capacity to have due regard for the rights of others

- How do we make sure we act in a way that acknowledges and respects the rights of others, in the same way as we expect them to respect our rights? What do we do when those rights conflict? What does 'do unto others as you would have them do unto you' mean in the context of rights and responsibilities? How do we deal with the protests of our children and others around us when they us denying their rights and acting in a manner which suggests: 'Do as I say, never mind what you see me do'?

Capacity to compromise, even when you're in the right

- Nothing prolongs conflict more than a refusal or incapacity to comprise. If we believe that to give an inch is a show of weakness and a transfer of power to the other, we displace all room for progress and for resolution of the problem. Sometimes, we box people in to the extent that they see no option to lash out, never mind that they might be the cause of the conflict. How can we feel confident enough to allow our opponent some space to retreat, some space to see how they might go forward out of the stalemate and not be totally crushed?

Capacity to keep the goal in focus and resist pressure to be like the rest

- Keeping the goal in focus means 'not cutting off your nose to spite your face'. It means giving way on the small things because you have greater things in your sights. It means not insisting on fighting, never mind winning, every single battle. It also means not allowing yourself to be distracted from what your main purpose is. It means persevering with the pain and the hardship in the full knowledge that the end is in sight, and when you reach your goal it will all have been worth every minute of it.
- This is yet another area where the example we show to our children is crucial. We need to discuss these matters fully and regularly with them, because the attitude they adopt would determine: their capacity to remain focused and motivated; their capacity to not allow themselves to get distracted by trivialities or by their friends' lack of focus. One young man said to me and a learning mentor recently, that he doesn't believe in this business of 'no pain, no gain'. As far as he was concerned, 'it stands to reason, no pain, no tears'. Needless to say, he passionately disagreed with my view that that was a recipe for mediocrity and a willingness to settle for anything but the best.

Capacity for deferred gratification: graft today, jam tomorrow

- This is another take on the 'no pain, no gain' philosophy, which so many of our children plainly reject. We live in a fast food, fast movies, fast success, culture. Some of us give in far too readily to our children and we encourage them to believe that it is unreasonable to make even the simplest demands of them. We work ourselves to the bone, feed them, clothe them, give them shelter, provide with every 'mod con' the electronic media tell them they need, and yet we treat them as if to require them to do some chores is a form of child abuse. We thus encourage them to make few demands of themselves. Consequently, children of high ability coast along, settling for mediocrity, and, in the case of boys, especially, adopt attitudes to self presentation that simply serve to mask their insecurity and lack of social and academic competence. In those circumstances, their masculinity becomes a weapon of power and dominance, a weapon they learn to use indiscriminately, even against their very fathers, mothers, and sisters. It serves them equally badly in school, in their relationship with their peers, in forming relationships and generally in their belief in what they are capable of in life.

The above factors are the result of reflection on the mediation and conflict resolution sessions I have conducted in a variety of settings over the last couple of years. I believe it sets out an agenda for us to follow as we seek to determine where our own values and principles come from, and, as parents, how we give expression to them and guide our children in adopting them.

It would be pretty obvious by now that all of the above have a bearing on our capacity to support our children's personal, spiritual, social and academic development, and to work in partnership with their school. It would be clear, also, that the home, school, peer group and community, all contribute to the development of those factors, factors which I see as reflective of: *values and principles of human conduct*

All four, home, school, peer group and community, contribute to building our capacity to engage with and live the values that make us fit for living in an ordered society and in an increasingly disordered world.

Home – School – Peer Group – Community
Each has a culture or cultures of its own. None of them operates in a neutral, value-free environment. Each has the capacity to engender behaviour that is conducive to harmony and order, as well as behaviour that is destructive and that detracts from the individual's capacity to act as a responsible social citizen. Each has the capacity to induce in the individual to a state of equilibrium and well being, as well as varying degrees of stress.

Intended outcomes
The sessions should:
- provide opportunities for participants to examine their own values base and the principles that govern their day to day living, as parents/carers and as students
- provide assistance with managing current conflicts, drawing upon the learning that all participants will have derived from examining

values and behaviours
- facilitate the development of models for resolving conflicts between groups of young people, between families and between young people/families and schools
- facilitate the development and trialling of models for resolving conflict in communities
- provide a support network for parents and young people, and particularly for single mothers parenting teenage children
- lay the foundations for the development of a confidential counselling and support service for young people living with bullying and in fear of crime

Recovery Strategies

Throughout our work, we will seek to devise strategies for supporting our young people's progress in schooling and education and reversing the persistent patterns of underachievement and under representation in key areas of the labour market, especially the professions. Strategies in relation to our communities:
- projecting high aspirations & high expectations as the norm
- combating the growing anti-learning culture amongst our young people
- reclaiming black youth culture
- getting more black young people into Higher Education than into Her Majesty's Prisons

Finally, in working towards a model for conflict resolution and peace building, we would address four principal themes, and they are:
1. Understanding Existing Conflict
2. Managing Conflict
3. Building on Progress
4. Sustaining Change, Avoiding Regression and the Recurrence of Conflict

In addition, we would agree methods for evaluating the application of the Model(s) and arrangements for ongoing capacity building and skills development.